BOULDER CITY LIBRARY
3 1432 00130 8806

D1123866

DK 24 HOURS

Desert

LONDON, NEW YORK, MUNICH,
MELBOURNE, and DELHI

Written and edited by Elizabeth Haldane
and Fleur Star
Designed by Mary Sandberg
and Cathy Chesson

DTP designer Almudena Díaz
Picture researchers Julia Harris-Voss
and Jo Walton
Production Lucy Baker
Jacket copywriter Adam Powley
Jacket editor Mariza O'Keeffe

Publishing manager Susan Leonard

Consultant Berny Sèbe

With thanks to Lisa Magloff for
project development

First American Edition, 2006
Published in the United States by
DK Publishing, Inc.
375 Hudson Street, New York, New York 10014

06 07 08 09 10 10 9 8 7 6 5 4 3 2 1

A Cataloging-in-Publication record for this book
is available from the Library of Congress.

ISBN-13 978-0-7566-1984-8
ISBN-10 0-7566-1984-X

Color reproduction by ICON, United Kingdom
Printed and bound in China
by L. Rex Printing Co. Ltd.

Discover more at
www.dk.com

Welcome to the Sahara,

6:00 am Dawn

10:00 am Morning

A desert might look like a vast empty space, but there's a lot of life among the sand and rocks. Spend 24 hours with some of the animals that live there and see how they survive in this dry, tough environment.

in Africa, an arid **desert** the size of Europe.

2:00 pm Afternoon

6:00 pm Dusk

10:00 pm Night

A **desert** is a place where only 10 in (25 cm) of **rain** falls in a year. Not many plants grow there.

Huge stretches of desert that are covered with sand dunes are called sand seas, or ergs.

In *24 Hours Desert* we spend a whole day in the Sahara Desert looking at the creatures that live there. During the day we return to the animals featured below to see what they are up to.

Only 15 percent of the Sahara is sand. The rest is made of up rocks and gravel.

Dorcas gazelle

At 3 ft (1 m) tall, a dorcas is the smallest species of gazelle. All species of desert antelope have amazing ways of coping with the dry desert.

Horned viper

Although just 24 in (60 cm) long, this snake has venom potent enough to kill a human being.

Camel

The 10 ft- (3 m-) long camel dwarfs all other desert animals. Saharan camels are dromedaries, a species with one big hump.

Scale Look for scale guides as you read the book. Based on children 3 ft 9 in (115 cm) tall, they will help you work out the size of the animals you meet.

Time to change

8:02 am Time sequence boxes show you how quickly things can change in the desert, whether at the oasis or in the middle of dunes.

The temperature in a desert can hit extreme highs, typically in the middle of the day in summer—but it can also plummet beyond freezing during the winter nights. It is lack of water, however, that makes a desert, not extreme temperatures.

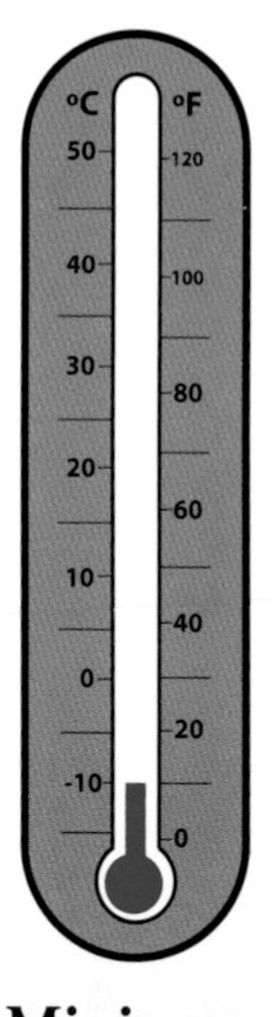

Minimum temperature
14 °F (-10 °C) —winter, nighttime

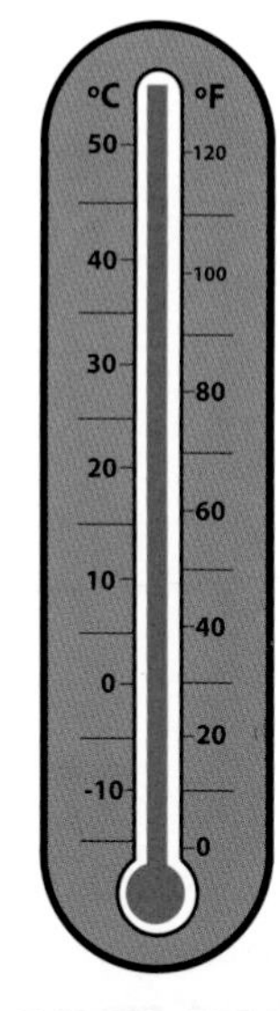

Maximum temperature
136 °F (58 °C) —summer, daytime

Fennec fox

The world's smallest fox is just 13 in (33 cm) long, but it has enormous ears! The fox loses body heat through its ears, helping to keep itself cool in the daytime.

Agama

The 12 in- (30 cm-) long common agama is also called the rainbow lizard because the males change color throughout the day.

The desert is quiet in the dawn chill, but in a few minutes it will be much busier.

The cold desert night comes to an end as the Sun rises over the sand dunes, bringing heat to the dry land. The daytime animals begin to stir; they need to get their food for the day before the desert gets too hot.

What's up at 6 o'clock

Fennec fox cubs are settling down to sleep in their den. They have spent the night feeding from their mother while their father was hunting.

As the Sun's rays heat the sand, the nocturnal **horned viper** finishes a night's hunting and warms itself before heading for bed.

A dozing, murky-colored **agama** sunbathes on a rock to raise its temperature. It needs to be warmed up before it becomes active.

In the morning the desert grasses and shrubs are heavy with dew. By grazing now, the **dorcas gazelle** takes in the moisture in the grass.

Already on the move, the **camel** has only had a few hours' rest overnight. It can keep active for 24 hours at a time, but will need to rest afterward.

It's hard to find water in the dry desert. Grazing mammals get moisture from plants when there is no water around for drinking. The best time for eating is first thing in the morning, when the temperature is cool and the grass is wet with dew.

Many desert animals, not just mammals, feed in the morning, before it gets too hot. A **darkling beetle** tips its head down to drink the dew off its own back.

Most of the Sahara's grazing mammals live in herds, and **sheep** are no exception. They live in the north of the desert, where it is a little easier to find food in the cooler mountains.

Camels have built-in pantries. Their humps contain fat, which they feed off when food is sparse. But they really load up when they find water, drinking up to a quarter of their body weight at one time and storing it in their stomachs.

Breakfast bar

Toward the edge of the desert, a rare **scimitar-horned oryx** finds a rich area of grass. These migrant mammals live in the southern Sahara when the rains are due, and move south to find food when it's dry.

Both the male and female addax have long, thin, spiraling horns.

The coat of an addax is white in the summer and turns brown in the winter.

A combination of being overhunted and lack of food due to drought nearly made the addax antelope extinct at one time. They are still very rare, but their numbers are growing.

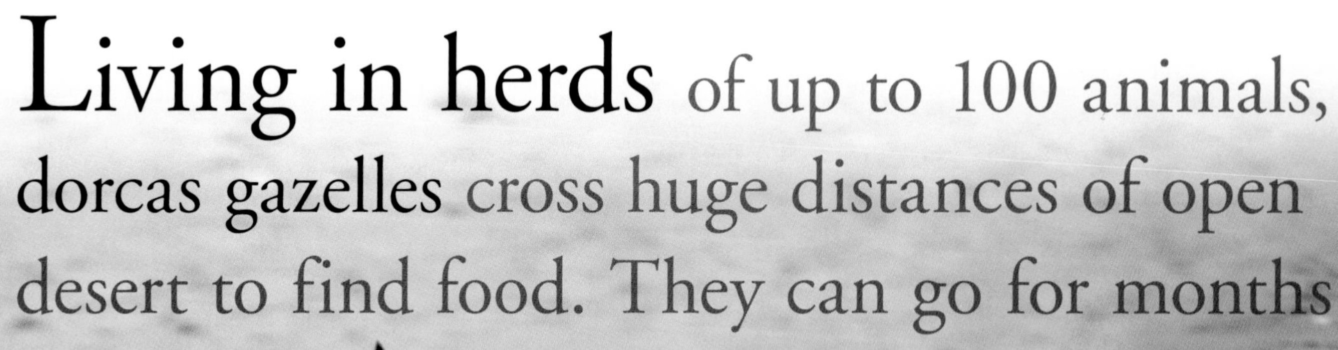

Living in herds of up to 100 animals, **dorcas gazelles** cross huge distances of open desert to find food. They can go for months without **drinking**, getting all their water from plants. The **lushest** plants grow at the edges of the desert.

Both male and female dorcas gazelles have horns. Those of females are thin and straight, but the males' curve backward and point up at the ends.

When startled, a dorcas calls through its nose to warn the herd. The call sounds like a duck quacking.

Graceful gazelles

If a predator strikes the herd, the gazelles **run away** at speeds of up to **55 mph** (90 kph).

Head to head

Male dorcas gazelles guard their territories fiercely, marking out areas with piles of dung and tussling with other males who overstep the mark. They also lock horns over potential mates. Females don't fight.

The smallest species of gazelle has the longest legs in relation to the size of its body—great for sprinting away from predators!

Like most desert animals, the rodents are foraging for food before the day gets too hot, when they head off to their burrows under ground. Small animals heat up quickly in the hot sun and lose body water if they are not in the shade.

Patrolling the desert skies, the golden eagle is a major predator of rodents, along with desert eagle owls and the rare Houbara bustards.

Gerbils have excellent hearing, which they use to detect predators and also to find mates. Being so small in such a vast desert, it can be hard for gerbils to locate each other.

Run, rodent, run!

9:09 am The nocturnal jerboa is finishing a night's foraging when it is disturbed by an eagle-eyed predator.

Of the 22 species of rodent living in the Sahara, half are gerbils.

The burrowers

The fat-tailed gerbil eats insects, which it routs out from the ground with its pointed snout.

Just as a camel stores fat in its hump, the **fat-tailed gerbil** carries its reserves in its club-shaped tail. Like many rodents, these gerbils have scent glands on their stomachs and mark their territories by rubbing their stomachs on the ground.

By far the biggest living thing on this page is the **euphorbia** plant, which can grow up to 10 ft (3 m) tall. The succulent plant takes in water when it rains and stores it in its leaves to survive dry periods.

The jerboa's name comes from the Arabic word *yerbo*, which means "big thighs". The jerboa also has a tail longer than its body, which acts as a prop when it sits still.

9:10 am With a leap of its huge legs, the jerboa springs into action and bounds away from the eagle.

9:10 am Despite being just 4 in (12 cm) long, the jerboa can leap up to 6 ft (2 m) in one jump, taking it safely to its burrow in a matter of moments. Made it!

The hind legs are four times bigger than the front legs.

The jerboa will spend the rest of the day asleep.

1 Desert shrub *Commosum calligonum*

A sudden wind appears and parts of the desert become a sandstorm as the fine, dusty sand is blown everywhere. Some winds gradually blow themselves out, but others stop as abruptly as this one has arrived.

What's up at 10 o'clock

Although some distance away, the **fennec fox** is woken by the sandstorm. Keeping its ears flat, it picks up the sound of the swirling winds.

The **horned viper** stays in its daytime bed, away from the sandstorm that could easily bury it. Its burrow was once made and occupied by a gerbil.

Away from the storm, the **agama** continues sunbathing. As the reptile warms up, it changes color from brown to blue and red.

The **dorcas gazelle** is caught unaware by the sandstorm. Sometimes hot air and lots of flies are blown in ahead of the storm, giving a warning.

Too big to hide, the **camel** keeps the sand at bay by closing its nostrils. It has extralong eyelashes and a third eyelid to protect its eyes.

Cold-blooded reptiles need to warm up before they start their day. They can stand the heat long after mammals have headed for shade, but will also take shelter when it gets too hot in summer.

A **chameleon** searches for insects to eat, its eyes able to swivel in different directions as it slowly paces the desert. It is not disturbed by the hot sand under its feet, even though it is more used to living in trees. Its split feet are ideal for gripping branches.

Desert monitors are the **biggest** reptiles in the Sahara. They swallow

The monitor's diet includes snakes and lizards—even those of the same species.

Agamas eat anything, from flowers to grasshoppers. This **desert agama** has wrestled with a scorpion, able to avoid its sting. But perhaps even more amazing is the agamas' trick of eating flies, which they catch in midflight by jumping into the air.

Lounging lizards

A skink's long, thin toes and pointed face are ideal tools for digging in the sand. The skink is also known as the sand fish because it moves around by swimming through the sand, hunting down insects found below the surface.

Desert monitors hibernate during the winter in shallow burrows that are not much bigger than themselves. They also burrow to avoid the strong summer sun around midday. If they get too hot, they die.

their prey **whole.**

Going, going, gone...

11:01 am While swimming for insects in the sand, the skink spies a predatory monitor lizard in the distance.

11:01 am Without hesitation, the skink takes a dive into the sand. Scales cover its ears to stop them from filling with sand.

11:02 am Seconds later the skink is well hidden, although it keeps a wary eye out for the danger to pass.

Common agamas inhabit rocky areas, rather than the hot dunes. They live in small groups, but it is easy to spot the leader: he's the brightly colored male among the brown females.

At one time,

ostriches lived in the wild in the Sahara. Now they live in the Sahel, the semidesert just south of the Sahara. It is a sign that the dry desert is spreading.

Spying a predator, an ostrich bends its neck to disguise itself. From a distance, the curled-up ostrich looks like a tree.

Who needs to fly?

Ostriches cannot fly, but they are the fastest animals on two legs, reaching speeds of 45 mph (70 kph) for 30 minutes at a time. Should a predator catch one, it will receive a nasty kick from the powerful bird.

Big birds

Ostriches are herd animals, but they do not just stick to their own kind. They often graze alongside herds of antelopes.

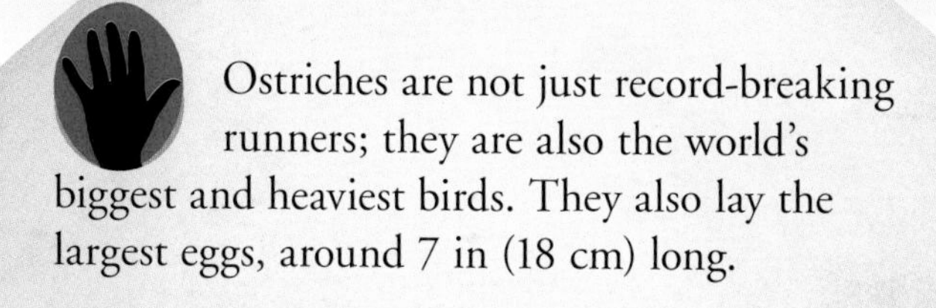

Ostriches are not just record-breaking runners; they are also the world's biggest and heaviest birds. They also lay the largest eggs, around 7 in (18 cm) long.

Laying all their eggs in one basket

12:30 pm A female ostrich guards her eggs in a shared nest. The male takes over at night, sitting on the clutch of 40–50 eggs.

40 days later The chicks begin to hatch. Only half the eggs will have survived to bear chicks.

This egg is **life-size**.

The chicks are already 1 ft (30 cm) tall at birth. Within a month, they can run with their parents.

One ostrich egg is equivalent to 24 chicken eggs—a good meal for predators such as this **Egyptian vulture**. The bird throws stones at the egg to smash its shell.

Caterpillar take-away

1:00 pm In one of their foraging expeditions, the ants sniff out the remains of a caterpillar. Within moments the whole troop is upon it.

1:10 pm The ants load up with chunks of grub and head back to the nest. By now the temperature is so hot, some ants will burn and not make it back.

The Sun is blazing, the summer heat is unbearable, but down among the sand grains there is still plenty of activity. Worker ants are out and about in the endless search for food for their queen.

Ants have five eyes. The three extras, in their foreheads, can see light patterns, which the ants use to find their way across the sand so they don't get lost.

There are 66 species of ant in the Sahara. Most live in underground nests, where there is some moisture, but some live in trees or near oases. Others inhabit dry dunes and rocks. Those that live underground are seed-eaters, carrying food to their nest in their jaws.

Sphinx moth caterpillars are also called hornworms because they have a horn on one end. The horn is harmless.

A **sphinx moth caterpillar** munches on euphorbia leaves, eating nonstop until it is ready to change into a moth. It was born in the tree so it could start eating straight after hatching.

Teams of dung beetles gather mammal dung and roll it home.

The tiny **seed bug** lives in many parts of the world. It hibernates during cold winters, but comes out to sunbathe when the weather is warmer. It feeds on plant seeds: at just ½ in (1 cm) long, an animal this small can eat only tiny portions.

Dung beetles may have an unsavory choice of habitat, but they make good use of their resources. They not only feed on the dung they collect from the desert mammals, but also lay their eggs in it.

1 Camel

Early afternoon is the hottest part of the day in the Saharan summer. There is very little action; those animals too big to hide from the heat underground seek out what limited shade the desert can offer.

What's up at 2 o'clock

The **fennec fox** has swapped its daytime burrow for a shady tree, its fur reflecting the heat. It even has furry feet so it can walk on hot sand.

Hidden under a rock, the **horned viper** faces a threat. It coils up and rubs its scales to make a warning sound; if that fails, it bares its fangs.

The **agama** is one of the few active animals, seeking out a mate. He has warmed up to full color, but the female remains brown all day.

The **dorcas gazelle** is conserving energy in the shade. Without this rest, it would not be able to live on the limited water it gets from its food.

Camels keep active for most of the day, so this baby takes advantage of the heat break to drink from its mother. It's also sheltered under there!

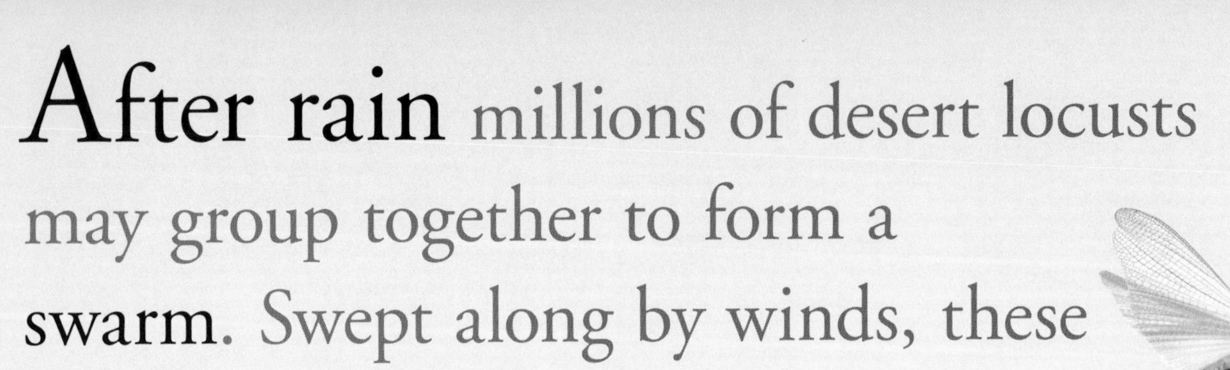

After rain millions of desert locusts may group together to form a swarm. Swept along by winds, these locusts will eat nearly every plant in their path.

Locusts that like to keep away from other locusts are called solitary.

Swarming locusts give off a special chemical that attracts other locusts.

A plague of locusts

The solitary (nonswarming) locust looks and behaves like a grasshopper. It flies by night.

Crowd behavior

When locusts crowd together, they change into gregarious or swarming locusts after four hours. They also change color.

The gregarious locust is pink at first and then becomes yellow when it is fully grown.

Desert locusts have been a serious pest since agriculture began.

Serious eaters

Each locust will eat its own weight in food each day. A swarm containing millions of insects can destroy crops and help to create famine.

Ponds and oases are the best places to see the variety of birds in the desert. Sandgrouse, desert larks, and wheatears are common locals; storks and swallows may be migrant visitors, while eagle owls and hawks are roving hunters.

White stork use thermals of hot air to help carry them across the desert.

A long way to go

Migrating birds are often seen crossing the desert. Among the largest are the white storks that leave Europe in the fall and fly over the Sahara to reach southern Africa for the winter.

Sandgrouse are found all over the desert, and will fly long distances to find water to drink.

Water transporter

These chestnut-bellied sandgrouse are well camouflaged against sand and vegetation. They fly in flocks to watering holes at dawn and dusk, where they drink and also soak up water in their soft breast feathers to take back to their chicks.

Desert eagle owls hunt rodents such as jerboas and gerbils, and even other birds.

Only adult male **wheatears** have this dazzling white crown.

Silent killer

The desert eagle owl's wings are designed for silent flight, making it a very effective hunter. Flying low over the ground, the owl is ready to pounce on an unsuspecting victim.

Sandgrouse are usually found in **flocks** of about **60 birds**.

Oases are fertile places in the desert where underground water comes to the surface. Sometimes the water appears naturally as a spring; but when it is 100 ft (30 m) below ground, it needs to be carried up to the surface through a well.

Water, water...
A flock of goats drink at a water hole. These ponds are made by underground springs or form after heavy rain. Some may last for three or four years.

Palm trees can grow 100 ft (30 m) tall and live for more than 100 years.

Tree of life

Every part of the date palm has a use. The fruit is a staple food for many desert dwellers. The large leaves are made into baskets, mats, and screens, and the wood is used for posts and rafters for huts. Any leftover wood is burned as fuel.

The ends of the leaves on the evergreen palm trees are razor sharp.

Fruits and nuts by the oasis

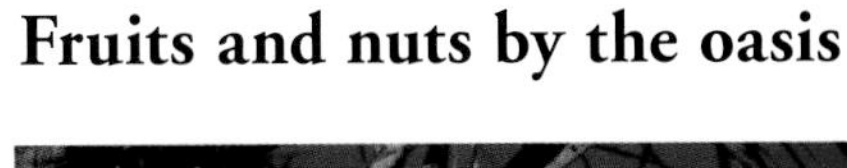

These dates are ripening in the sunlight. A large bunch like this can contain more than a thousand dates.

This is a fruit from a pomegranate tree. The brilliant red pulp covering the seeds inside is edible.

Wild desert melons grow in seasonal riverbeds. They are not edible: their juice is very bitter and they are poisonous to humans.

Pink blossom covers these almond trees, which are grown as a crop at many oases. They need much less water than cereal crops.

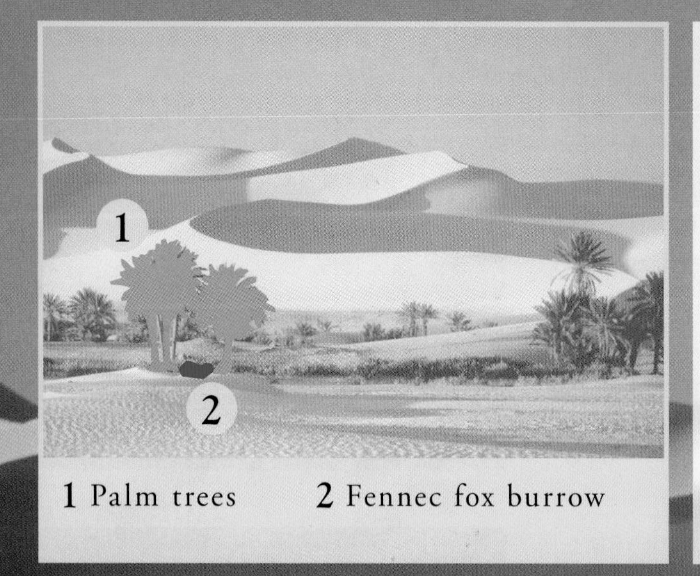

1 Palm trees 2 Fennec fox burrow

With sunset comes cooler temperatures, bringing a burst of activity to the desert. Diurnal, or daytime, animals come out of the shade to hunt for supper, while the nocturnal ones are waking up for the night.

What's up at 6 o'clock?

The **fennec fox** emerges from its burrow, ready to start hunting. It is careful to look and listen for predators such as eagles and hawks.

Just becoming active, the **horned viper** side-winds across the sand. It moves its body quickly, one part at a time, so it has less contact with the hot sand.

The hungry **agama** polishes off an evening meal of a small gecko. This is a large meal: it mostly feeds on insects such as ants and locusts.

During the hot summer months, the **dorcas gazelle** continues to rest until nightfall. It scrapes the sand with its hooves to make a smooth bed.

Resuming its journey across the open sand, the **camel** looks for grazing places. It will munch for several hours on any shrubs it may find.

Camels are often called ships of the desert because they are so well designed for life in a dry environment and can easily carry heavy loads.

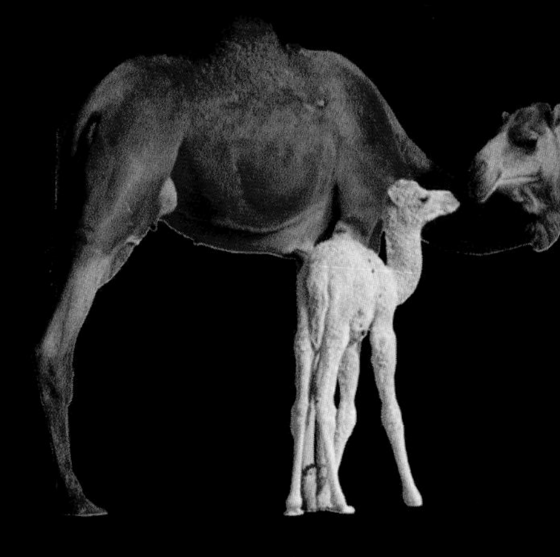
A baby camel stays with its mother for two to three years.

Captive camels

There are no wild camels left in the Sahara—only domesticated ones. They are well cared for and are taken to wells to drink and to grazing areas to replenish their fat stores.

Ready, set, up!

1 A camel rests with its legs tucked under its body.

2 The camel rises by first getting into a kneeling position.

3 Then the camel pushes up with its back legs.

4 Finally, the camel straightens out its front legs.

5 The camel is up on all fours and ready to go.

If a camel's hump leans to one side, it has used up its fat reserves.

A male camel gets very defensive during the mating season.

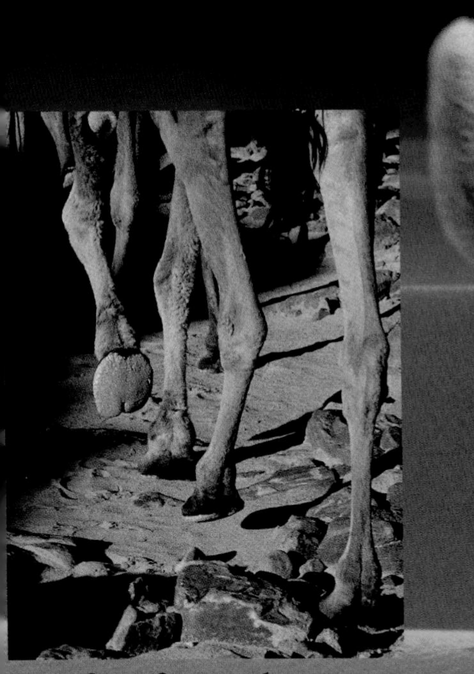

Best foot forward
Camels' feet are ideal for crossing the dunes. Each foot is split into two pads that do not sink into the sand nor slip on flat rocks. The soft pads also act like shock absorbers.

Under cover of darkness, when it is much cooler, a cheetah prowls around looking for a meal. Moving in, a pair of golden jackals waits to scavenge the cheetah's kill—if it's been lucky enough to find any prey.

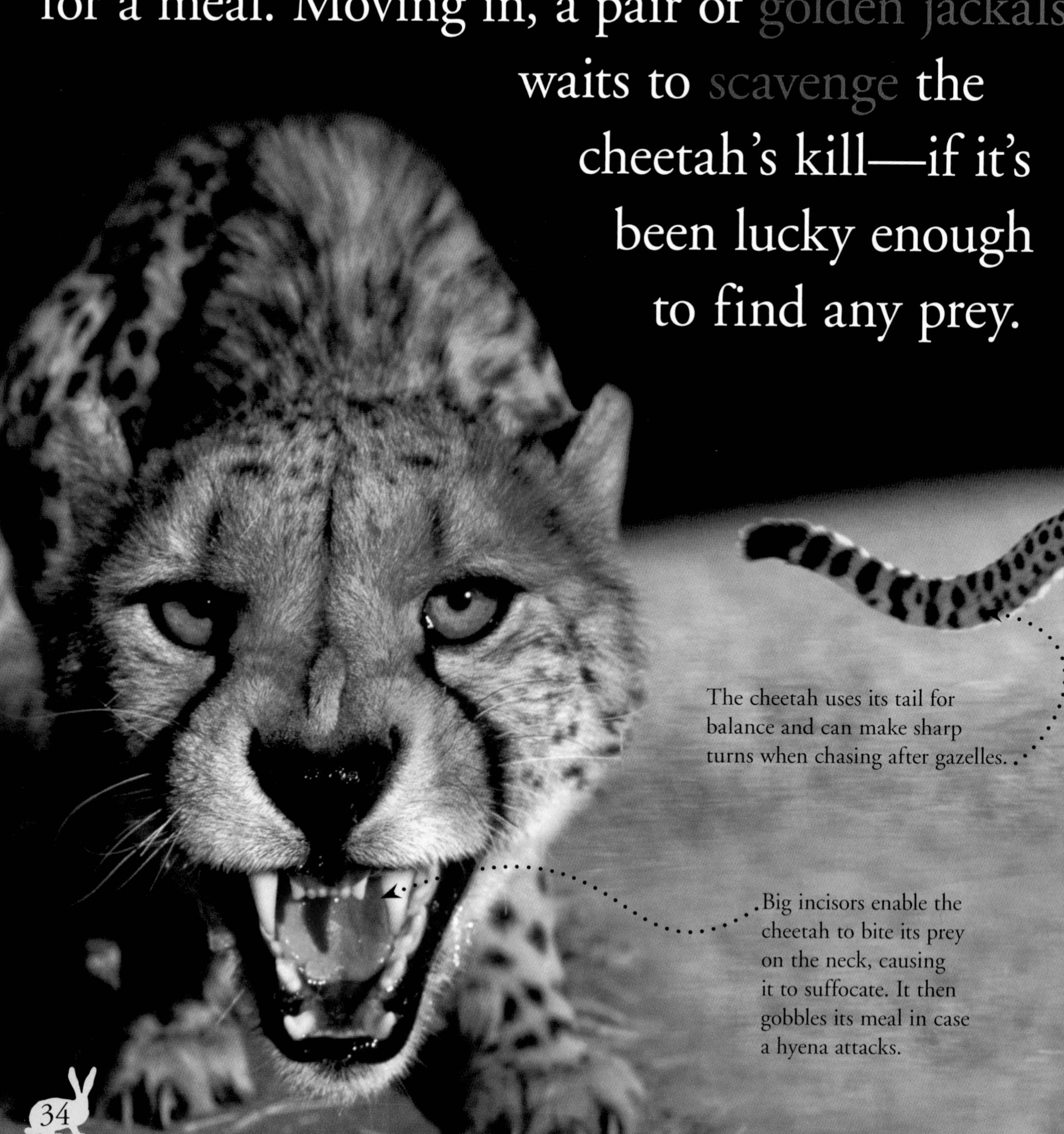

The cheetah uses its tail for balance and can make sharp turns when chasing after gazelles.

Big incisors enable the cheetah to bite its prey on the neck, causing it to suffocate. It then gobbles its meal in case a hyena attacks.

Fastest feet on Earth

Cheetahs hunt either by stalking their prey to catch it unawares or by sprinting after it at high speeds. They are the fastest of all land animals, reaching 60 mph (100 kph)—but only for short distances.

Running at 55 mph (90 kph) the cheetah will be taking an incredible three and a half strides per second.

A changing menu throughout the night

In the cool of the early morning, **dorcas gazelles** are easy prey, especially those too young and small to run with the herd.

Cape hares are nocturnal targets. They can put up a good chase, making sudden turns, and leaping up to 12 ft (4 m) in one bound.

Sniffing around a carcass, a golden jackal is looking for parts of the prey that other scavengers have left behind. Its mate is nearby, and together they will take home food for their young by regurgitating what they have eaten and feeding it to the pups.

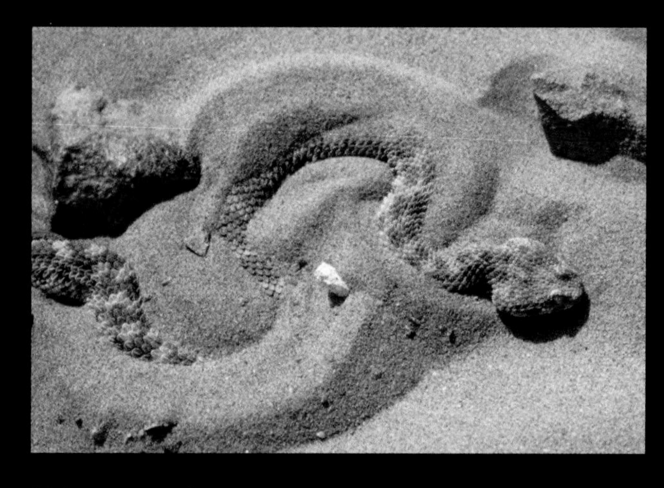

Disappearing act
The sand viper shuffles down into the sand by rocking its body from side to side. It shovels sand over itself as it submerges. This squat snake will soon be almost completely hidden and ready to strike an unsuspecting victim.

Look out small rodents,

mammals, and birds because on warm nights the snakes come out looking for a meal. The horned viper and its close relative the sand viper may cover a large area on their hunt. They will leave zigzag tracks in the sand.

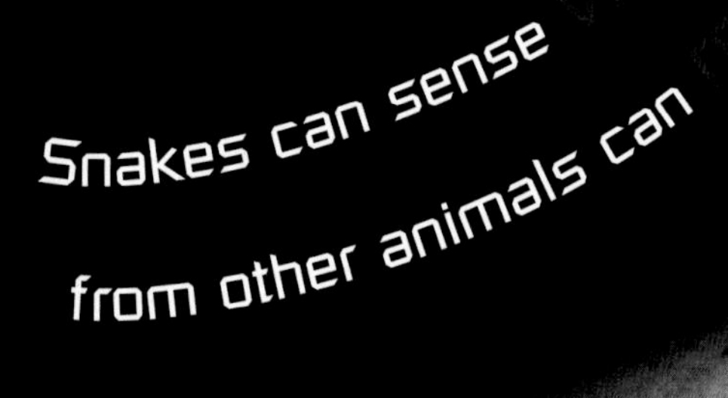

Snakes can sense vibrations in the air, so the slightest movement from other animals can reveal the location of potential prey.

The sand viper's light, mottled skin makes it hard to spot against sand. The waterproof skin helps the snake retain moisture in the desert heat.

Venomous vipers

As the horned viper lies ready to ambush its prey, all that can be seen are its thornlike horns and catlike eyes. It will attack with an open mouth and stab the animal with its long fangs.

Biting off more than you can chew

8:29 pm The horned viper has killed a bird by injecting venom into it. Now it has to eat it!

8:37 pm Like all snakes, the horned viper can dislocate its jaws, allowing it to swallow prey wider than itself. Nearly half the bird is now inside.

8:47 pm Ten minutes later, the bird is passing slowly down the snake. It will take several weeks for it to be digested.

Slither, slide, strike...
In the enveloping darkness the sand viper is out hunting. Its fangs are folded back into its mouth and will only be brought out for biting.

1 Desert eagle owl

Night brings cool air to the desert. In winter, the temperature can fall to below freezing, yet many desert animals are active at night. It is much easier for furry mammals to keep warm at night than cool in the day.

What's up at 10 o'clock?

The **fennec fox** senses prey, hearing the slightest movement with its huge ears. It also has good night vision for spotting larger animals.

The **horned viper** hides underground to ambush unsuspecting prey. It lunges, bites, and kills with the poison stored in venom sacs near its fangs.

As the air cools, the **agama** fades back to its less colorful skin. It will spend the night with its family group, hidden among the desert rocks.

Dorcas gazelles are diurnal, but in very hot weather they are active during the night. If rain has fallen, a large herd gathers to feed on plants.

The **camel** has a thick wool coat to keep it warm during the cold night. In summer, when the coat molts, the camel stores heat from the day.

On the alert, the sand cat looks around carefully before leaving the safety of its burrow to hunt. It can travel as much as 5 miles (8 km) in a single night, searching for prey by walking and listening.

When threatened, sand cats will crouch beside a small rock or tuft of grass. One of the pair pictured here is looking as fierce as it can.

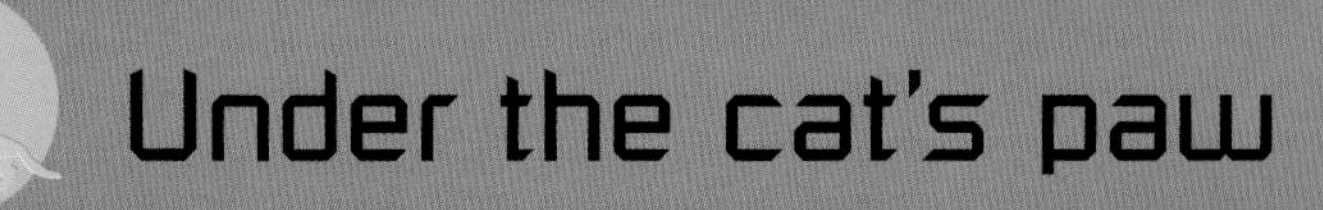

Under the cat's paw

It's snake for supper

A sand cat will attack a poisonous snake. This one is about to whack a horned viper over the head with its paw. It will then bite through the snake's neck to kill it.

Pounce, kill, play...

5:02 pm Crouching low, a sand cat waits beside a jerboa's burrow. It may return to the burrow at night hoping to catch one of the occupants.

11:36 pm In the cool of the night a jerboa is out looking for food. A sand cat is about to pounce and will kill it with a quick bite through its neck.

6:22 am The sand cat plays with the dead jerboa before munching it. Water from the body gives the sand cat the moisture it needs.

A female fennec fox stays home with her young cubs while the male goes out hunting. It takes little time for these expert diggers to create their underground dens. They are kept very clean and neat, and provide a safe and cool daytime retreat.

Just popping out for a meal

6.00 pm As dusk falls and the air begins to cool, the foxes wake up and the male emerges.

6.05 pm After a quick check for predators, the male starts to look for food to take back to the female in the den.

7.00 am The fox makes one last hunt before it gets hot. He may stay out of his den during the day, returning tonight.

What big ears they have.... And they are all the better for hearing prey, even underground.

Between a rock and a hard place

Out in the open, the foxes face predators such as birds of prey. Their pale, sandy-colored fur provides some camouflage, but it is safer to hide inside a cave or in crevice among the rocks.

The foxes' diet includes moisture-rich plants, eggs, and birds such as the sandgrouse...

... And any animal small enough for them to catch. Lizards and desert locusts make a crunchy snack!

Small rodents, such as gerbils, are pounced on much like a cat catches mice.

Feeding the family

Fennec fox cubs feed on their mother's milk until they are one month old. Once they are weaned, the male will stop bringing the female food and she leaves the den to hunt for herself.

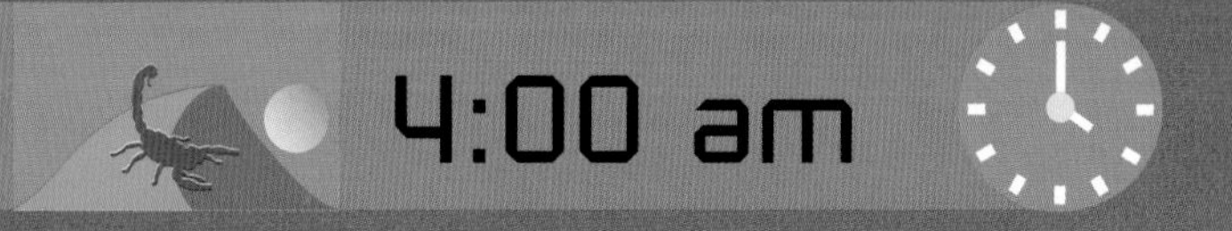

Scorpions are probably the oldest stinging things in existence. They stay hidden under rocks or in burrows during the day and come out at night to hunt—as does the fast-moving camel spider.

Multiple birth

Scorpions give birth to up to 100 live young. The newborn scorpions climb up their mother's legs and onto her back. They stay there until their first molt a few days after their birth.

The babies get a ride until they can fend for themselves.

The yellow scorpion has the strongest venom of all scorpions and is very quick to sting. The pincers are used to hold prey.

A sting in the tail

The sting is as sharp as a needle.

Venom-injecting sting at the end of the tail.

Deadly injection

The scorpion has pushed its tail downward to pierce the skin of the gecko and inject its deadly venom. It now holds the gecko in its pincers and starts to tuck in. It won't need to eat for a while after this feast.

Shedding its skin

A young scorpion sheds its skin in a safe hiding place. Before molting, its blood pressure increases, making the old skeleton crack. Scorpions usually molt six times before they are adult.

When it has molted, the scorpion is soft-bodied and needs to hide until its new skeleton has hardened.

Camel spiders can give a nasty bite. They have very strong jaws for their size.

Looking like a big hairy spider, this strange beast known as a camel spider is actually neither spider nor scorpion. A fast mover—it can reach 10 mph (16 kph)—it feeds on insects, lizards, small mammals, and birds.

Glossary

Here are the meanings of some of the important words you will come across as you read about deserts and the animals that live there.

ARID Another word for "dry." Arid regions have little water.

BURROW A hole in the ground that an animal lives in. It is also the action of digging the hole.

CAMOUFLAGE The color or pattern of any living thing that blends in with its surroundings, so it can't be seen.

COLD-BLOODED Animals that warm up or cool down depending on the temperature around them. Reptiles are cold-blooded.

DESERT An area that gets very little rainfall. Not many plants grow in deserts because of the lack of water.

DIURNAL Animals that are diurnal are active during the daytime.

FERTILE When something can produce fruit, it is fertile. Ground that is fertile is good for growing plants.

FORAGING Searching for food, particularly plants.

GRAZE To feed on grass or other plants.

HERD A group of animals, such as gazelles.

MIGRATION When animals move from one part of the world to another to find food or shelter when the seasons change.

MOLT To shed feathers, hair, or skin in the process of growing.

NOCTURNAL Animals that are nocturnal are active during the nighttime.

OASIS A fertile area within a desert. Oases usually have a pool of water surrounded by trees.

POTENT Another word for "strong." A snake might have very potent venom.

PREDATOR An animal that hunts, kills, and eats other animals.

PREY The animal that is hunted, killed, and eaten by a predator.

SAND DUNE A hill of sand that has been blown into shape by the wind.

SCAVENGER An animal that eats leftover meat from another animal's kill.

SWARM A large group of insects, such as locusts.

THERMAL A current of warm air that rises. Birds sometimes ride thermals to gain height in the sky or use less energy in flight.

VENOM A poisonous liquid that snakes and scorpions have. They bite or sting prey to inject venom and kill the prey.

WARM-BLOODED The opposite of cold-blooded. Animals that keep their body temperatures at a constant level. Mammals are warm-blooded.

Picture credits

The publisher would like to thank the following for their kind permission to reproduce their photographs:

(Key: a-above; b-below/bottom; c-center; f-far; l-left; r-right; t-top)

Alamy Images: Jon Arnold 2-3b; Blickwinkel 15ca, 23cra; Gary Cook 17br; Robert Harding World Imagery 1; David Hosking 10, 41tr; Iconotec 22-23; ICSDB 11bl; Juniors Bildarchiv 4-5c; Malie Rich-Griffith 43tr; David Sanger 11br; Ismael Schwartz 3tl; David J Slater 31crb; **alsirhan.com:** 41cr; **Ardea.com:** Ian Beames 31tr; Ken Lucas 9tl; **www.geres-asso.org/Michel Aymerich:** 36tl, 45cr, 45bl; **Eyal Bartov:** 13bl; **Raymonde Bonnefille/ sahara-nature.com:** 20bl, 21tl; **Corbis:** 4tl, 23cr; Craig Aurness 15br; Frans Lemmens 24-25; Photowood Inc. 3tc; G. Rossenbach 5tr; **DK Images:** courtesy of Berlin Zoo 40tl; **fjexpeditions.com/Andras Zboray:** 25tr, 36-37, 37tr, 37cr, 37br; **FLPA – images of nature:** Chris Mattison 4br, 7ca, 37tl; Mitsuaki Iwago/ Minden 18bl, 19ca; B. Borrell Cascals 29cra; Gerry Ellis/Minden 20br, 32tr; Yossi Eshbol 7t, 40bl, 48; David Hosking 9bl, 13tl, 42bl; E. & D. Hosking 4bl; Mark Moffett/Minden 8tr; Hans Schouten 26tr; Sunset 19cb; Duncan Usher 27tl; Konrad Wothe/Minden 8b; **Foto Natura:** Konrad Wothe 26-27; **Getty Images:** Frans Lemmens 3tr, 16tl; National Geographic/Michael Melford 7c; National Geographic/Michael K. Nichols 39crb; National Geographic/Carsten Peter 7br, 39br; **Robert Harding Picture Library:** 5br, 39cr; **ImageState/Pictor:** Philippe Saharoff/ Explorer 32-33; **Lonely Planet Images:** Olivier Cirendini 13r; **N.H.P.A.:** 26c; Martin Harvey 9br; Daniel Heuclin 12br, 13br, 16bl, 17tr, 17cra, 20-21, 39cra, 42-43, 44c, 45tl; Karl Switak 17crb; **Natural Visions:** 16-17; **naturepl.com:** Hanne & Jens Eriksen 26, 31br; Karl Ammann 19br; Neil Lucas 31cra; Vincent Munier 18-19; Jose B. Ruiz 29tr; Anup Shah 18tr, 31cr; **OSF/photolibrary. com:** Eyal Bartov 42cl, 42clb; Waina Cheng 15crb; Alain Dragesco-Joffe 35cr, 35br, 40-41, 41tl; IFA-Bilderteam Gmbh 44b; Manfred Pfefferle 27tr; **Science Photo Library:** Alan and Sandy Carey 34-35; George D. Lepp 15cr; **Alain Sèbe & Berny Sèbe/www. alainsebeimages.com:** 2tl, 2tr, 6-7, 8c, 14-15, 27cr, 28tr, 28-29, 29crb, 29br, 33cl, 44-45; **Still Pictures:** Martin Harvey 34l; Alain Dragesco-Joffe 15tr, 23tr, 23crb, 27cl, 35t, 41br; Patricia Jordan 33br; Frans Lemmens 23br, 43br; Roland Seitre 11t; **Erwin & Peggy Bauer/Wildstock:** 43tl